France Gagnon Pratte
Robert W. Sandford

Chateau Lake Louise

A Diamond in the Wilderness

Chateau Lake Louise
Canadian Pacific Hotels

Éditions
Continuité

Canadian Cataloguing in Publication data
Gagnon Pratte, France

The Chateau Lake Louise: a diamond in the wilderness

Includes bibliographical references.

ISBN 2-922527-00-X (pbk.)
ISBN 2-922527-01-8 (bound)

1. Chateau Lake Louise (Alta.) – History. I. Sandford, Robert W. II. Title.

TX941.C432G34 1998 647.947123'32 C98-941471-X

PROJECT DIRECTOR: France Gagnon Pratte
AUTHORS: France Gagnon Pratte - Robert W. Sandford
PROJECT COORDINATOR: Louise Mercier
RESEARCH: France Gagnon Pratte
COPY-EDITING AND PROOF READING: Linda Blythe
BOOK DESIGN: Norman Dupuis
COVER PHOTOGRAPH: CP Hotel Archives
ELECTRONIC PRE-PRESS: Compelec inc.
PRINTER: Imprimerie La Renaissance inc.

Produced exclusively for Canadian Pacific Stores Limited

ISBN 2-922527-00-X (soft cover)
ISBN 2-922527-01-8 (hard cover)

Legal deposit - National Library of Québec, 1998
Legal deposit - National Library of Canada, 1998

Acknowledgements

Dedication

For Amery Jane,

child of the high mountains

R.W. Sandford

For Julien,

a budding mountaineer

France Gagnon Pratte

There are many individuals whose help and enthusiasm made this book possible. First and foremost, David Bayne, General Manager of Chateau Lake Louise, and the hotel's public relations people who provided us with archives, photos and memorabilia that were essential. In Montreal, Nancy Williatte-Battet from the Canadian Pacific Archives staff was indispensable in finding photographic and archival material relating to Lake Louise and its Chateau.

We also feel that it is important to acknowledge a number of previous works on the history of the Canadian Pacific Railway and Canadian architecture which helped us understand the role played by Lake Louise in the history of Canada. Books by Harold Kalman, Pierre Berton, Jon Whyte and Carole Harmon, E.J.Hart, Walter Vaughan and others provided the historical background.

Finally, we would like to express our gratitude to Linda Blythe for editing, Norman Dupuis for book design and Louise Mercier, Director of Les Éditions Continuité, for coordinating the whole project.

(CP)	Canadian Pacific Archives
(CPH)	Canadian Pacific Hotel Archives

Table of Contents

CHATEAU LAKE LOUISE
CANADIAN PACIFIC
HOTELS

Over the past century, Canadian Pacific hotels have played an important role in the shaping of Canadian history and culture. Nowhere is this more true than in the Western mountains where Canadian Pacific was a partner in the development of the country's first national parks. The Chateau Lake Louise is a particularly important property in that it is widely regarded as an icon of Canadian landscape heritage and national identity. The Chateau is a symbol of the unique relationship Canadians have with their remarkable national park landscapes and the pride they take in sharing them with visitors from all over the world.

Canadian Pacific Hotels Ltd. recognizes its responsibility for the preservation and celebration of its unique heritage properties. By protecting and sharing our natural and cultural heritage, we hope to distinguish ourselves as Canada's leading heritage hotel chain.

Bill Fatt
Chairman and CEO
Canadian Pacific Hotels

Foreword

Chateau Lake Louise is more than a grand hotel. Since 1890, it has played a central role in the evolving history of Canada's mountain West. As early as 1893, the hotel was a centre for mountaineering and tourist adventure in the remote and largely unmapped West. In 1899, Canadian Pacific imported the first professionally trained mountain guides to lead guests from the front steps of the hotel to the summits of their dreams. These Swiss mountaineers taught thousands of locals and visitors how to climb and, later, to ski. The Swiss influence on local architecture and cuisine can still be felt at Lake Louise today.

Now a National Historic Site, Chateau Lake Louise remains a centre for landscape experience in Banff National Park. By demonstrating stewardship and accurate interpretation of our heritage assets, by educating our employees about the significance of Canadian Pacific's role in shaping Canadian history, and by providing our guests with opportunities to learn about natural and cultural heritage, we hope to be worthy partners in sharing this National Historic Site with the world.

David Bayne
General Manager
Chateau Lake Louise

Mountain trail riders at Lake Louise; painting by an unknown artist (CP)

A Diamond In The Wilderness

The Great Divide is the spine of Western North America. This divide marks the birthplace of rivers. Watersheds along this great wall stand back to back. It is here that water ceases its westward flow to the Pacific and begins its life-giving journey east to the Great Plains. Amidst this spectacular confusion of bare rock, scree and ice is Lake Louise. Over all the high Rockies there is no place like it. No matter how many times mountains rise and are slowly worn away, it is unlikely this awesome scene would be created again. Six glaciers pour into the head of a spectacular valley. The valley widens into broken moraines and is cut by high saddles that form passes between it and other remarkable valleys around it. In a great bowl carved out by millions of tons of slowly moving ice is the lake itself. Lake Louise is a natural glory: a liquid jewel in a frozen ocean of stone. Its waters reflect the massive walls that surround it. On its northern shore is a grand hotel—Chateau Lake Louise.

Early poster of Chateau Lake Louise Canadian Pacific Rockies (CP)

Chateau Lake Louise is unique. It is part of a spectacular landscape and a remarkable history. Certainly quality and excellent service are important here, as they are at all grand hotels, but something more is required of a place so intimately tied to the delicate beauty around it. It is to experience this wilderness heritage that visitors flock to the lake. The lake's beauty will fill you, perhaps even capture you, and over all your life you will not forget what you saw here. The hotel and its setting are one.

To visit Chateau Lake Louise is to participate in history. The lessons the lake teaches begin with the history of the planet itself. There is no better place to see and feel the forces that have shaped and reshaped the face of the earth. There is natural history here. A green surf of plants and remarkable animals washes upward from the lake pushing life's limits toward the cold summits above. There is native history here. Peoples travelled through these valleys for hundreds of generations before the arrival of the first Europeans. There is railway history at Lake Louise. It was over Kicking Horse Pass that the first transcontinental railway was constructed. If the wind was right, the lonely whistle of the steam train could be sometimes heard from the shore of the lake. The train brought the first tourist-adventurers. Among these were a few who would become explorers. Mapping and photographing as they discovered the glory of the lake and the surrounding valleys, the first tourists made history their own.

There is also a mountaineering history associated with Lake Louise. The peaks above the lake are the birthplace of a Canadian passion for climbing. There is national park history at Lake Louise, for the lake and its environs are part of Banff National Park and a larger United Nations World Heritage Site that encompasses other important reserves along the spine of the Great Divide. There is also

(CP)

architectural history at Lake Louise. From its inception as a tiny chalet to its grand restoration and completion more than a century later, Chateau Lake Louise is one of Canada's most important buildings. There is also a proud history associated with the people who have lived and worked at the great Chateau. It is to the people who have made this hotel what it is today that this book is ultimately dedicated.

For nearly a century a Canadian Pacific hotel has stood on the shores of Lake Louise. The Chateau has presided over the history of the lake with elegance and grace. It has watched over a view that is famous the world over, a panorama that has come to symbolize the magnificent heritage enjoyed by Canadians and their guests in the Rocky Mountains.

CHAPTER I

The Canadian Rockies

ke Louise,
inting by
Malczewski
P)

Native peoples were the first human cultures in what is now Banff National Park. It is amply clear from early accounts that Native groups visited the valley of the Kicking Horse River and its tributaries only seasonally. Used principally as a summer hunting ground, this high, wild country was simply too severe to survive in during the winter. Native peoples preceded Europeans in the Rockies by thousands of years and knew the country intimately. The Shuswap Indians travelled widely along the western edge of the Great Divide, as did the Kootenays. Both of these groups, as David Thompson indicates in his journals from the early nineteenth century, appear to have made regular spring and summer journeys over various passes into what is now Alberta.

The first generation of explorers in the Canadian Rockies missed Lake Louise completely. They were too busy delineating the topography of the main valleys and searching for passes to spend much time exploring side valleys walled in by peaks and glaciers.

Canada at Confederation was a disjointed country to say the least. Just as now, settlement was concentrated in Upper Canada in Ontario and Quebec. The only other large concentration of people was along the Pacific coast. To achieve greatness, central Canada had to embrace the west coast by way of the almost limitless lands that formed the interior of the continent. Four years after Confederation, the Dominion of Canada made a rash proposal to the Colony of British Columbia, offering it a railway in exchange for political union.

With the laying of the rails, Canada's mountain West was altered quickly and completely. Primeval valleys shuddered with the dull roar of exploding dynamite. The ringing of the hammers on cold steel drowned out the gurgle of stream water, and valleys, inhabited for centuries by only the rocks and the trees, were animated anew by the eerie whistle of the steam train. In the noise, the confusion, and the politics, Native peoples were soon forgotten.

Donald A. Smith driving the last spike in the railway linking east and west on November 7, 1885, referred to as the Great Canadian Photograph. (CP)

Van Horne portrayed by G. Marengas (CP)

Even with the railway completed, the Canadian West was still a wild place. A few metres from the tracks the wilderness marched off up roaring creeks and rivers. It did not take long for even the most casual railway passenger to understand that the route the trains took through Canada's Western mountains was an incursion into a vast unknown. The fact that the Canadian Pacific Railway successfully advertised wilderness as an attraction is an important development in its own right. That the land, brutal, remote and dangerous, was the greatest obstacle to the building of the railway that made Canada possible. Now those same qualities were being touted as the reason for coming to this far-off, exotic land. The enlightenment of a century before had borne healthy fruit. It was now de rigueur to seek beauty and peace in the silence of remote places. It also brought one a certain amount of personal status to have done so.

Thomas Wilson and the Stoney Indians who discovered Lake Louise in 1882 (CP)

The Discovery of Lake Louise

In the summer of 1882, young Thomas Wilson was employed at the Canadian Pacific Railway, ferrying supplies and equipment for the crews working at Kicking Horse Pass. One fateful, rainy day, as Wilson huddled around a big fire with a group of Stoney Indians heading for Morley and camping with him, he heard the distinct roar of avalanches nearby. With the help of the few Indian words he had picked up as well as some sign language, he was able to determine that the snowslides were occurring on "snow mountains above the Lake of Little Fishes." When it was still drizzling the next day, Wilson decided to take the day off and asked the Stoney Edwin Hunter, whose Indian name meant "gold seeker," if he would take him to this lake. Hunter was happy to oblige and off they went: Wilson, Hunter and another Indian friend. They worked their way there on horseback without any trouble since the vegetation was fairly light on the eastern slope of the mountain. When they came upon the lake, Wilson was captivated by its unparalleled beauty. According to his account, they then sat and smoked and gazed at the gem of a beauty beneath the glacier. It is best to hear his reaction first-hand:

Princess Louise, Queen Victoria's daughter (CP)

As God is my judge I never in all my explorations saw such a matchless scene. The surface of the lake was still as a mirror. On the right and left, forests that had never known the axe came down to the shores, apparently growing out of the blue and green water.

The background, a mile and a half away, was divided into three tones of white, opal and brown, where the glacier merged with the shining water. The sun, high in the noon hour, poured into the pool, which reflected the whole landscape that formed the horseshoe.

He renamed it Emerald Lake for the shining colour of its water and he himself became known as the first white man to see it. Emerald Lake was the name that appeared on the first geological map for this part of the Rockies, drawn up by George Mercer Dawson from data compiled between 1881 and 1884 and published in 1886. The name Laggan Lake was also used, because of its proximity to the CPR's Laggan Station. When Tom Wilson returned to the site in 1884, he found that the lake reflected the blue sky and decided that the name Emerald Lake was inaccurate. He changed it to Lake Louise in honour of a member of his party who was travelling with her father, Sir Richard Temple, from the railway station up into the mountains. Later, the Geographical Society of Canada officially named it Lake Louise, but after Queen Victoria's fourth daughter, Princess Louise Caroline Alberta.

Tom Wilson went on to live in the mountains for the rest of his life. In time, he became the most famous outfitter and guide in the Rockies, the man to see if you wanted access to the wilderness that surrounded Lake Louise.

Lake Louise, painting by Franklin Arbuckle (CP)

Lake Louise, painting by M.H. Roberts (CP)

CHAPTER II

Humble Beginnings

In November 1885 at Craigellachie in Eagle Pass, the last spike was driven in the new Canadian railway line that linked the country's eastern shores to its west coast, uniting nine Canadian provinces to make one nation. The builder of the railway and "railroad general", William Van Horne, envisioned wealthy Europeans and Americans touring the Canadian Rockies, climbing the peaks and exploring rivers and gorges.

That year, only a dozen people came to Laggan Lake. In 1884, members of the British Association for the Advancement of Science had been among the first mountaineers to climb the Lake Louise area and to write about it. Two of them, Reverend Henry Swanzy and Irish Clergyman William Spotswood Green, became instrumental in opening Victoria Glacier and the area to tourism. In 1888, Swanzy and Green came back on a trip to the Selkirk range in the Rockies. Green described Lake Louise in these words:

> I was quite unprepared for the full beauty of the scene. Nothing of the kind could possibly surpass it. I was somewhat reminded of the Oeschinensee in Switzerland, but Lake Louise is twice as long, the forests surrounding it are far richer, and the grouping of mountains is simply perfection.

Returning east, Green and Swanzy made a point of meeting with CPR President William Van Horne in order to impart their enthusiasm. Van Horne was in the process of developing a vast advertising campaign to lure foreigners and Canadians into the heart of the Canadian Rockies and to the Canadian Pacific hotels in the mountains. After Green's visit, Van Horne wrote to Canadian Pacific Superintendant William Whyte to tell him that Lake Louise, near Laggan, was probably the most interesting spot on the line. In this letter to Whyte, he adds:

> ... Not far from Banff, it will afford a very desirable place for excursions from the Banff Hotel... It might be well to put up a chalet and provide some boats there. I would be glad if you would look into this matter before winter sets in and ascertain what the expense of making a road would be, and find a good location on the lake for a chalet. We would have to provide a few sleeping bunks and a small kitchen as a good many visitors would probably stay overnight.

For a whole year Van Horne, Vice-President Shaughnessy, Superintendent Whyte and Passenger Agent David NcNicoll discussed ideas and plans for building a guest house at Lake Louise. Then, in 1890, a small building was put up close to the spot where Green had first gazed upon the lake. It was built on the shoreline, amidst bogs and brush.

The one-storey log cabin was fifty feet long by thirty feet wide under a long sloping roof. It provided shelter and included two small bedrooms and a kitchen. A central area served as office, dining room, bar and gathering place. There was a breathtaking view of the mountains through large windows taking up most of the wall facing the lake.

The first Lake Louise Chalet (CP)

The early log chalet on the shores of Lake Louise (CP)

For three years, the little chalet hosted visitors from different dining stations as well as from the famous Banff Springs Hotel. The site could be reached from Laggan Station by foot or on horseback. There were not all that many visitors to the lake but enthusiastic travellers came to fish or climb the surrounding mountains.They would take the train to Laggan Station then walk over rough terrain along the creek to the shining lake or use a horse and carriage provided by the chalet's manager, Willoughby Astley.

This small cabin was the first in a series of buildings culminating in the the grand Chateau Lake Louise of today as well as a tribute to Van Horne's vision of tourism in the Rockies. The Lake Louise Chalet was the CPR's first attempt to exploit the tourist potential of the mountain wilderness away from the main line.

Considering the extraordinary hotel it had built at Banff in 1888, the Canadian Pacific Railway Company took a decidedly rustic approach to the development of the Lake Louise area. The chalet and site were better suited to lumberjacks than they were to elegant guests who returned every season.

Many problems assailed visitors to Lake Louise. The extensive correspondence in the CP's archives attests to the company's diligence in responding to complaints, however. It reacted promptly, for instance, to this letter from a Mr. Henderson to President T.G. Shaughnessy:

In the early 1890's the Chalet became the meeting place for mountaineers and trekkers (CP)

It is undoubtedly the finest scenery of the kind on the CPR at present known. The road there is atrocious and the mosquitoes at the house on the lake beyond any I ever saw, even at Sicamous. A short distance round, they were scarce and the reason is that the house is surrounded by a peat bog full of water, like a sponge. It should not take much to obviate this—some draining and filling. As it is, life is a burden there and will be for five or six weeks.

Immediately, the Lake Louise manager was informed of this guest's remarks. Shortly after, improvements were approved, including a decent road from the station to the lake, horses and carriages, and also a fence to keep the horses from wandering.

The original chalet burned down on June 19, 1893. For the next few months, visitors to Lake Louise had to camp on the lakeshore. The building had been insured for two thousand five hundred dollars and the CPR decided not to spend any more than that on the new building.

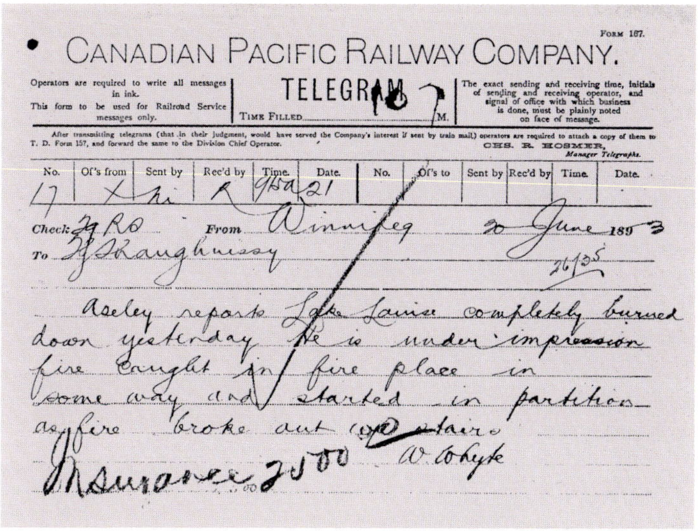

FORM 167.

CANADIAN PACIFIC RAILWAY COMPANY.

Operators are required to write all messages in ink.
This form to be used for Railroad Service messages only.

TELEGRAM

TIME FILLED 10 7 M.

The exact sending and receiving time, initials of sending and receiving operator, and signal of office with which business is done, must be plainly noted on face of message.

After transmitting telegrams (that in their judgment, would have served the Company's interest if sent by train mail) operators are required to attach a copy of them to T. D. Form 157, and forward the same to the Division Chief Operator.
CHS. R. HOSMER, Manager Telegraphs.

No.	Of's from	Sent by	Rec'd by	Time.	Date.	No.	Of's to	Sent by	Rec'd by	Time.	Date.
17	X	Mi	R	9Ba	21						

Check: 29 RO From Winnipeg 20 June 1893
To TG Shaughnessy
26/35

Aseley reports Lake Louise completely burned down yesterday He is under impression fire caught in fire place in some way and started in partition as fire broke out upstairs
Insurance 2500 W. Whyte

Telegram from manager Whyte to CP president Shaughnessy announcing the fire at Lake Louise and mentioning the amount of the insurance (CP)

The new chalet, which was further back from the lake, opened in 1894. It was a two-storey cabin with clapboard and rustic verandas on the outside, and could accommodate 15 to 20 guests. As an added attraction, an "easy riding" wagon was provided to convey passengers from Laggan to the lake and a path was cleared for those who were more adventurous and chose to hike over from the station.

After the 1893 fire, the CPR built a second Chalet at Lake Louise (CP)

The following year, an upper storey was added. Also, the grounds were improved and the bog filled in. A large living room served as an office and dining room. Its large windows offered a magnificent view of Victoria Glacier. There were seven small bedrooms for the more fortunate guests and others were offered tents on the grounds.

Lake Louise was already attracting the Banff Springs Hotel's international clientele, who would come to the lake by train, sometimes for afternoon tea. By the end of the century, the chalet at Lake Louise had become quite popular. Initially, CPR executives responded to the demand for additional space by providing tents for visitors, then it had more chalets built around the original site.

The addition of a second story to the Lake Louise Chalet provided more rooms for guests (CP)

To get tourists to use his railway line, Van Horne promoted the Canadian Rockies. The CPR published all sorts of advertising literature vaunting the merits of hiking, horseback riding, fishing, mountain climbing and touring in the Rockies. The new Banff Springs Hotel, designed by New York architect Bruce Price and inaugurated in June 1888, offered a wide range of activities to an affluent clientele. In one of the CPR's first pamphlets, published in 1895, *Canadian National Park: Glaciers and Mountain Ranges of British Columbia,* a visit to Lake Louise was described as a must.

> The drive is two and one-half miles through a pine forest, in which a good carriage road has been cut. Although the most graphic word painting does not adequately convey the effect of the approach to Lake Louise and its sudden burst on the sight of the traveller, for mental pictures involve themselves with actual sights, it may be worth while quoting one writer: "Nestling at the foot of two great mountains which seem to guard against the encroachments of the vast glaciers resting on the sides of a third, canopied by a sky like the petal of a soft blush rose, its unfathomable waters reproducing, with mirror-like fidelity, the green forests, bare peaks and motionless seas of snow-mantled ice—Lake Louise is a dream of loveliness."
>
> On the margin of the lake the railway company have built a chalet, at which visitors rest and lunch. It is not precisely a hotel, though rooms and meals are provided for those who desire to remain either to fish or hunt—the region abounding in mountain goat and numerous coveys of ptarmigan grouse—or to explore the mountains. Ponies can be hired at the chalet for the ascent to Lakes Mirror (altitude 6,480 feet) and Agnes (altitude 6,801 feet) by those not desiring the walk, but the delights of mountain climbing are here lavishly offered. Experienced guides may also be secured. Conveyances will meet the train at Laggan and, by pre-arrangement, the round trip, including the ascent to the upper lakes, can be made from Banff in one day.

Colour publicity for Lake Louise (CP)

In the same pamphlet, the CPR advertised its three mountain chalet hotels, Mount Stephen House at Field in the Kicking Horse Valley, Glacier House at the foot of Illecilliwaet Glacier and Fraser Canyon House at North Bend. The rates were $3.00 per day.

Van Horne's prophecy that "since we cannot export the scenery, we will have to import the tourists" became reality. While only fifty guests registered at the first chalet on the shores of Lake Louise in 1890, by 1912, 50,000 guests had slept there.

As early as 1896, alterations were made to the cabin and other major improvements were under way. Guests were soon pleased to discover a rustic bridge spanning the outlet of the lake, a boathouse and wharf, a stable for 8 horses and a wagon shed for 2 wagons. There was also a bathroom with a 500-gallon water tank in the attic for domestic purposes and a 3,000-gallon tank for general use. In addition, a hydraulic ram could pump 3,000 gallons in 24 hours. The Laggan station grounds were revamped too and a single telephone line was installed between Banff and Laggan. Altogether, these improvements cost the CPR $1,900.

Lake Louise, Laggan. Early postcard (CP)

Early view of Laggan Station (CP)

Manager Astley fishing at Lake Louise (Whyte Museum of the Canadian Rockies)

A Chalet Grows up to be a Chateau

Glacier House built for the CP by Thomas Charles Sorby (CP)

Three years later, further changes had become imperative. The CPR decided to commission architect Thomas Charles Sorby to enlarge the building.

Sorby had designed the three dining stations in the Rockies: Mount Stephen House, Fraser Canyon House and Glacier House. They all had three storeys, were gabled, and were flanked by a two-storey wing on one side, with hall, office and kitchen, and a single-storey wing on the other, with a dining room. The wood frame was clad in horizontal siding, except for the central gable where the wall projected slightly and was shingled—probably to suggest the appearance of a Swiss chalet.

Sorby was commissioned by the CPR to incorporate a structure similar to that of the dining stations, and Glacier House in particular, with the Lake Louise Chalet. He built a large two-storey structure with open verandas around the original rustic chalet. Inside, there were beamed ceilings, polished floors and large picture windows with a "million-dollar view."

By 1899, the Sorby building was already obsolete and the CPR decided to enlarge the chalet once again. The railway company hired Francis Mawson Rattenbury to undertake a complete overhaul of the building. This architect also worked on a 54-room wing at Glacier House and on the famous Empress Hotel in Victoria during the same time period.

Sorby's work at Lake Louise (CP)

Riders preparing to leave the Rattenbury wing (CP)

A series of alterations were built between 1900 and 1912 by architect F.M. Rattenbury (CP)

Between 1900 and 1912, Rattenbury designed many additions for Lake Louise as the number of guests grew. He began his work on the Sorby structure with a large three-storey addition complete with all sorts of Victorian touches, including a large gable, corner turrets and bargeboards. He then built a large wing which formed a T with the original 1894 building and was also decorated with turrets, gables and big verandas. After that, he added a second storey with six dormer windows. The next enlargement contrasted sharply with the existing wooden structure and consisted of a very austere, two-storey boulder wing with low roofs and large picture windows looking out over the lake. A few years later, this stone wing served as a foundation for a large gabled extension entirely decorated in mock Neo-Tudor style with high roofs and pointed dormers. A new wooden addition with large picturesque verandas was also Neo-Tudor, but on a smaller scale. By then, the eclectic and irregular new hotel decorated in the fashionable Neo-Tudor style was very impressive.

Large extension in mock Neo-Tudor style built by Rattenbury. The center portion is built on a former two story boulder wing. (CP)

Built in the centre of the complex, perpendicular to it, an immense addition made the structure now look like a huge T, with the bar of the T fronting the lake.The Lake Louise Hotel was quite an eclectic mix, reflecting many different periods of construction while attempting a unified look with the Neo-Tudor design of the facades. The overall effect was certainly picturesque to say the least and it seemed to please the hotel's affluent clientele. The lakefront facade built from the original chalet was a composite of many styles, what with its turreted addition and the boulder construction serving as a foundation for a Neo-Tudor building. The end portion was a picturesque and somewhat better-designed wing with large verandas. The design was considered curiously charming. It looked somewhat like a number of wooden constructions that had been put together at random, gabled and half-timbered. It suited the landscape surprisingly well.

The completed T-shape wooden structure at Lake Louise before the building of the Painter wing (CP)

Rattenbury's design for the Lake Louise Chalet conserved part of the mountain dining station look and added some touches inspired by the chateau style of the Banff Springs Hotel and the Chateau Frontenac in Quebec City. He also added conspicuous Tudor elements such as the false half-timbering referred to as Tudor Revival—decorative vertical boards set against the plain walls. This was a relatively new style in Canada and part of the revivalist movement in architecture.

Lake Louise Chalet interior around 1906 (CP)

Lake Louise Chalet interior around 1906 (CP)

Lake Louise Chalet interior around 1906 (CP)

The Painter Wing

Walter S. Painter was born in Reading, Pennsylvania in 1877. He came to Canada in 1901 and designed the Russell Theatre in Ottawa, the auditorium and opera house in Quebec City, a theatre in London, Ontario, and a number of theatres in the United States. He opened a short-lived practice in Toronto under the name Brown and Painter. In 1905, he was named chief architect for the Canadian Pacific Railway. The CP hotels in Montreal and Vancouver, the Empress Hotel in Victoria, and several train stations, such as the Windsor Station in Montreal, were among his accomplishments. He also enlarged the Hotel Palliser in Calgary and designed the Banff Springs Cave and Basin swimming pools and buildings.

Painter's contributions to the Chateau Frontenac and the Banff Springs Hotel were remarkable. Immediately after he left the CPR, he started working on the Chateau Lake Louise (1912) and the Hotel Vancouver. Painter later returned to Banff, where he retired in 1957.

Architect Walter S. Painter added a contrasting modern wing to the Lake Louise Chalet in 1920 (CP)

Architect Walter S. Painter added a contrasting modern wing to the Lake Louise Chalet in 1912 (CP)

In 1912, a large addition of at least 350 rooms was needed for the guests, who had often been refused a room for lack of space. The CPR chose architect Walter Painter to undertake this project and approved his plans for a major extension of the hotel.

Painter and Sir Thomas Shaughnessy were already corresponding regularly in 1906 to discuss details of the new wing. The design took more than six years to complete since construction only began in 1912. The proposed annex was a concrete wing that would enable the hotel to accommodate up to 400 guests at a time. It featured an immense hall with huge glass windows overlooking the lake and a ballroom 180 feet long.

In sharp contrast to the Neo-Tudor design of the old chalet and its many additions, the new wing had flat unornamented walls flanked by two projecting towers. Painter drew his inspiration from the Empress Hotel in Victoria but made his design more subdued. The new wing had a flat roof and no pointed dormers. Its flat-arched "loggia"—actually the dining room windows in this case—between two towers, was reminiscent of that of the Empress.

Painter's centre wing at the Banff Springs (which he also built in 1912) had taken the chateau style in a Scottish Baronial direction. The building at Lake Louise was definitely nothing like a French chateau or Scottish castle, however. It was closer to a huge pseudo-Renaissance, or Palladian, villa. Although the contrast with the wooden chalet surprised many people, it did not keep them away. Of course, the elegant interiors and superior cuisine helped lure them back...

The architecture of the new wing was influenced by the Italian Renaissance (CP)

The entire ground floor of the new wing was taken up by a spacious dining room. Great windows looking out over the lake made it one of the most splendid dining rooms that could be imagined outside an artist's dream. Above it, there were four bedroom floors which brought the total guest rooms to an amazing 320. The ballroom was built in the dining room of the old wing.

During this same period, in 1912, a tramway line was built from the train station to the hotel. Not only did it provide easy access to the new Chateau for guests, it was also an economical way of moving construction materials for the new Painter wing. At first, the only passenger car was an open-air model but a closed car was soon added for night traffic. As many as 180 passengers could take the tram to Lake Louise daily at a fare of fifty cents per person. In its first year in operation, 32,500 guests used it. The line had its own flat car, dump car, locomotive, self-powered passenger cars, and a turntable for cars at the end.

In 1912, a tramway line was built from the train station to the hotel (CP)

A New Look

July 3rd, 1924; the hotel staff lost all their possessions but saved the guests' belongings (CP)

At the hotel, the new arrivals would walk to the hotel over a covered platform. In 1925, the original equipment was supplemented by two additional passenger cars. This time, they were closed vehicles and very much like streetcars. They made as many as thirty round trips daily. The Lake Louise Tramway stopped operating in 1930 and the rails were removed the following year.

It is significant that in 1925 the Laggan station was renamed Lake Louise Station and that a new road was built from Banff to Lake Louise as part of the transcontinental highway.

Getting back to the hotel itself, by 1916-1917, the CPR had added a powerhouse on Louise Creek, one kilometre downstream from the lake, to serve the new dining room in the Painter wing.

Then, in 1924 disaster struck.

At 2:38 in the afternoon on July 3rd, a telegram was sent to the company president by manager Whyte. It read as follows: "Chalet Lake Louise on fire and am advised beyond control."

The immense wooden building vanished in just a few hours. The Painter wing was saved, however, by closing the metal fire screens that separated it from the Rattenbury wings and tearing down the arch connecting them.

It was truly a disaster. The hotel staff, losing all their possessions in the process, saved the guests' as well as the hotel's. In true Canadian Pacific spirit, it was "business as usual" soon after. The CPR set up the front desk in the Red Hall and dinner was served to 126 guests as of six o'clock, with the orchestra playing as usual and the regular dance from nine until eleven!

Reconstruction began almost immediately. The hotel had to be ready to open for the next season.

The wooden Chalet was completely destroyed in the 1924 fire (CP)

The Montreal architects Barrott and Blackader were commissioned to rebuild the hotel. Instead of reviving the picturesque wooden structure that had burned down, they designed an extension of the Painter wing in the same Italianate style. The walls were flat and unornamented with projecting towers topped by a high roof. Criticism from Parks Canada officials about the lack of "chateauesque" detail prompted the architects to add rows of dormer windows, providing the only ornamentation below the roof, and large covered loggias at ground level. Unlike the Banff Springs Hotel and the Empress Hotel, the massive structure built on the shores of Lake Louise did not blend in with the surrounding landscape. But the view from the Chateau of the mountains, glaciers and shimmering lake was nothing if not breathtaking!

November 9th, 1924, the new Chateau Lake Louise taking shape (CP)

The general contractors chosen for the job were Carter Hall Aldinger Co. Ltd from Winnipeg and the general building inspector was H.S. Bare. There were a number of unusual conditions that needed to be overcome in order to build such a large building during the winter in this isolated locality. Lake Louise is a

A roofed and weather-tight structure of lumber and building paper around a steel frame was put up to form a shell so that the construction work could be done during the winter months (Dominion Bridge collection)

(Dominion Bridge collection)

mile above sea level and winter temperatures often plunge to 40 degrees below zero. In order to build during the winter months, all materials and supplies — about 30,000 tons of them — had to be transported four miles (6,4 km) from the main line over a narrow-gauge track, the hotel tramway line, a long stretch of which had a 4-percent grade. What is more, it soon became evident that the construction work had to be done inside a temporary heated shell.

A roofed and weathertight structure of lumber and building paper around a steel frame was put up. High-pressure boilers were then installed with thousands of feet of steam pipes and a lighting system so that the workmen could work at a temperature of 45 degrees above zero when it was 40 degrees below zero outside. Construction companies from the U.S. were paying special attention to the progress of this project because of the implications that the building industry could be active 12 months of the year.

The first phase, which consisted of excavation work, started on September lst, 1924, but not many men could be employed until September 15th when the hotel closed for the season. The hoarding was put up as fast as the building of the steelwork would allow, and suspended forms for the concrete floors were also built right behind the steel workers. About 10,000 feet of 1 ¼-inch heating coils were installed and connected to the boiler house but, as the weather got colder, three temporary boilers were hooked up. As soon as possible, the permanent radiators in the rooms were connected because the construction of the exterior walls prevented a lot of heat from the coils from penetrating inside the building. Also, additional heat was required to dry out plaster and for other reasons.

The tramway line moved construction materials for the new Painter wing. It was shut down in 1930 (CP)

The floors were made of reinforced concrete. It was discovered that the extra thickness on the rough floor called a finishing coat would not survive in an unheated building so the whole thickness of the floor had to be poured and finished at once. Eight floors were poured in seventeen days.

The new extension was a fireproof, steel frame (9,400 tons) and reinforced concrete building. It had tile floors; concrete, brick, stone and stucco walls; tile partitions; a sloping copper roof and a flat tar roof. The finished floors were of quarry tile in the main rooms, with Tyndall stone interior trim. The materials used came from all over Canada: the Tyndall stone, which is full of beautiful fossil forms, was brought in from Manitoba; asbestos gravel for the walks came from Quebec; and British Columbia supplied its finest woods.

Two additional storeys of bedrooms had to be installed over part of the existing concrete wing. Also, many alterations had to be made to the old wing adjacent to the new extension so that the new building would line up.

Practically all the work inside and outside of the building was finished before the shell enclosure was removed. The building was completed in every detail, the furniture in place, and the hotel ready for guests on June 1st, 1925. The grounds were graded and planted and no evidence of construction remained.

The building was 52 feet wide, 285 feet long and 125 feet high. There was a basement, ground floor and eight bedroom floors. Each guest room had its own private bathroom.

The new Chateau Lake Louise attracted an international clientele and became one of the major attractions in the Rockies (R.W. Sandford collection)

The tall windows in the lounge looked out on a magnificent vista of Victoria Glacier (CP)

A large covered porch led from the station to the entrance of the main building. The rotunda, a room 38 feet wide by 80 feet long, faced the lake, as did the adjoining lounge. Opening off the lounge was the main office as well as the bank, information office, ticket office, telephone, entrance to elevators, and the news and curio stand. A stone staircase 10 feet wide led up from the lounge to the main dining room, located in the existing fireproof wing. This staircase served a mezzanine floor with the ladies rest room and a doctor's office. Additional staircases were built at each end of the building. Finally, there was a grand ballroom 36 feet by 70 feet which opened out onto a loggia and balcony.

The ballroom decorated in soft colours boasted a sophisticated five-piece orchestra (CP)

The luxurious lounges were all refinement and beauty, reflecting a tradition established by decorator Kate Reed wife of CP manager Hayter Reed (CP)

This famous poster depicting "Beautiful Lake Louise" lured visitors from the world over (CP)

CHAPTER III

The Golden Years

Watercolours by artist R.H. Palenske illustrated the 1929 pamphlets for the Chateau Lake Louise (CP)

In the Challenge of the Mountains, the best and most comprehensive advertising booklet produced by the CPR at the turn of the century (and posted around the world at the cost of a 4-cent stamp), Chateau Lake Louise, the "most winsome spot in the whole Canadian Rockies," was described in glowing terms:

> Everything about the Chateau is in good taste. The rooms are large and airy, the service is excellent and the cuisine perfect, and the view from the broad verandas across the flower decked lawns is captivating in the extreme. The Chateau is open for guests from June 10th till September 30th, the rates being $4.00 per day and upward.

(CP)

Early poster of Chateau Lake Louise (CP)

Watercolours by R.H. Palenske (CP)

Lake Louise was promoted as the best attraction near Banff and "a spot so beautiful that no one who visits the Canadian Rockies can afford to miss seeing it." The Chateau Lake Louise mostly attracted a young, affluent and international clientele who came year after year for two or three weeks at a time. It was frequented by famous mountain climbers from abroad, movie stars on their honeymoons, painters and writers from all over the world, and travellers en route to and from the Orient. These people would explore the valleys around the lake, climb the peaks, take walks, and go on pony trips and fishing excursions.

By 1927, the CPR had more than a hundred miles of trails in the area, with three teahouses and cabins. Those who opted for the mountaineering experience could make use of tents, mountain huts or small cabins, but they were always delighted to return to the incomparable luxury of the Chateau. With its vast interiors, opulent lounges, high picture windows, rich marble floors, antique furniture and bronze chandeliers, it made quite a change after the wilderness.

And there was so much to do... On the front terrace, amidst a riot of yellow and orange poppies, there was a lovely swimming pool shielded from the breeze by a glassed-in colonnade but open to the rays of the warm sun from above. This pool, built in 1926, was 110 feet long and 40 feet across and the second largest in Canada. At one point, the famous swimmer Olaf Andersen worked there as the lifeguard. Just before tea time or after a game of tennis or a long ride, the swimming pool was the most popular place in sight.

A remarkable pamphlet from the thirties waxes poetic about the Chateau experience:

The Chateau is always alive with light, music and gaiety. Lounges are crowded with bridge-parties, groups in deep chairs and sofas watching the smartly dressed people, listening to the dance music. Come out into the lounge-like loggia, and down through the terraced garden into the magic Alpine night. Drift in enchanted silence over the velvety upturned sky trailing hands that dip up liquid stars and cut a flaming wake through the path of the moon. Or stroll the scented forest path around the far curve of the lake and watch the Chateau lights wink out.

The hotel truly sparkled at night, when animated men and women in their elegant evening dress would sail down broad stairs and through luxurious lounges.

The Chateau lounge (CP)

Watercolours
by R.H. Palenske (CP)

The luxurious chateau service extended even to the pool area (CP)

(CP)

A pool a hundred feet long was built in 1926 with the famous swimmer Olaf Andersen as lifeguard (CP)

The ballroom opened off the main lounge and boasted a sophisticated five-piece orchestra. It was decorated in soft colours, with deep chairs and palms. There was also a very popular billiard room called Down by the Tavern. Cozy nooks off the lounges were often chosen for quiet card games and illustrated lectures were held regularly in the lounges for the guests' edification.

Chateau evenings sparkled, as women in beautiful evening gowns sailed down broad stairs and through luxurious lounges (CP)

Dancing at the chateau was still popular in the 40's. (CP)

The poetic pamphlet quoted above also has a lot to say about the atmosphere at breakfast, lunch and dinner time:

> Well, if this isn't starting the day right! Fancy coming down to breakfast and finding a golden room flooded with sunshine, fresh Alpine flowers on the tables and a glacier through the window. Victoria is the most friendly glacier you ever saw. Victoria smiles perhaps because she is framed in softly wooded slopes and bathed in sunlight all day long.
>
> Lunch time finds the dining room cool and the lake a bowl of living color, blending, shifting, changing: emerald and sapphire, topaz and turquoise, jade and amber and lapiz lazuli. At dinner time a cosmopolitan crowd gathers in a room brilliant with light, poppy coloured lamps glowing in the alcoves, the great stone fireplace blazing and crackling.

The Chateau was luxurious in service and appointments. Half of its 386 rooms and suites faced the lake and its incredible setting and all had great double windows looking out at the majestic mountains. The spacious and charming guest rooms featured long mirrors, easy chairs, twin beds of luxurious softness, writing desks and private baths—truly homes away from home. Every possible convenience and service was provided: beauty parlour and barber shop, nursery, doctor's office, ticket office, post office, public stenographer, photography studios.

(CPH)

The interior decor of the hotel was influenced by other Canadian Pacific hotels, such as the Chateau Frontenac in Quebec City, which had recently been decorated by the Montreal architect William Maxwell, the Empress Hotel in Victoria, and also the Banff Springs Hotel with its new tower and completely revamped rooms. The elegant interiors, furniture and appliances, and silver and china were all chosen with care and in keeping with a tradition established by Mrs. Kate Reed, the wife of CP hotel manager Hayter Reed. As early as 1894, she was recognized as being the main inspiration behind all the hotel decors, and in 1901 she was commissioned to decorate the royal train that would carry the Duke and Duchess of Cornwall and York across Canada on a CPR line. The elegance, distinction and refined atmosphere of the CPR properties owed a great deal to her.

Kate Reed had decorated the Lake Louise Chalet and won world acclaim for her taste. She was consulted whenever colours were to be chosen or furniture, silver or china to be purchased for the new Chateau Lake Louise. The interior was all refinement and beauty, and guests from all around the world flocked to this shimmering lake nestled in its decor of wild poppies.

Romantic Publicity for the CPR (CP)

(CP)

Royalty, Movie Stars and Other Notables

Right from the start, life at Lake Louise meant mountain climbing, horseback riding and contemplating nature. Lake Louise was one of the most popular climbing areas in the Canadian Rockies. Alpinists from all over the world flocked there year after year and the Swiss guides had their headquarters near the Lake Louise chalet.

October 1894, Lady Aberdeen sketching the mountains at Lake Louise (CP)

In 1886, Lady Agnes MacDonald accompanied her husband Sir John A. MacDonald, the Prime Minister of Canada, on his first visit to Western Canada. She caused quite a stir when she insisted on riding the engine cowcatcher from Calgary to Laggan. Lady Agnes returned to the Rockies and stayed in a small cabin near the Banff Springs Hotel during the summers of 1887, 1888 and 1889.

On October 18, 1894, Lady Aberdeen spent some time at the Lake Louise chalet and enjoyed sketching the mountains and flowers thereabouts. She wrote extensively about her travels in the Canadian Rockies. One of her better known travel diaries is "Through Canada with a Kodak."

In September 1919, the Prince of Wales and future King Edward VIII visited Lake Louise and Lake Agnes. The Prince apparently went up to take tea in the Lake Agnes Tea House "during his morning exercise." More recently, King Hussein and Queen Noor of Jordan paid a visit in 1989.

In September 1919, the future Edward VIII stopped at Lake Louise and Lake Agnes (CP)

These famous people became fervent admirers of Victoria Glacier. As ambassadors, they travelled the world and imparted their love for the Canadian Rockies.

The Canadian Rockies made an ideal setting for Hollywood movies. Film producers and stars, from John Barrymore to Clint Eastwood, were attracted by the majestic mountains, shimmering lakes, easy locations and great hotels.

Mary Pickford and Douglas Fairbanks were visitors to Lake Louise (CP)

Regional director Ted Kissane at Lake Louise gala with actor Christopher Reeves (Photo: Timothy Reynolds)

In 1944, Son of Lassie *was filmed at Lake Louise and Moraine Lake (CP)*

Famous actress Angie Dickinson with maitre d'hotel Mike Langlois at Lake Louise gala (Photo: Timothy Reynolds)

In 1928, a film crew was in Lake Louise shooting Ernst Lubitsch's *Eternal Love* featuring John Barrymore and Camilla Horn. Lake Louise became a place in Switzerland for the occasion. Barrymore played a daredevil hunter with two women vying for his attentions. One of the women, played by Miss Horn, was the spiritual type while the other, Mona Rico, was a "spitfire girl." The most memorable scene in the movie is the one in which Barrymore and Horn are caught in an avalanche and die in each others' arms.

In 1951, Princess Elizabeth and Prince Philip crossed Canada by train and visited the Rockies (CP)

In 1944, *Son of Lassie* was filmed at Moraine Lake and Lake Louise. The movie starred Peter Lawford and was about an R.A.F. pilot and his ever-present collie Lassie. By 1920, the first film had been produced there: *Cameron of the Mounted*. In 1924, *The Silent Partner* starring Mary Astor was also produced, in part, at Lake Louise.

Mary Astor skijoring at Lake Louise during filming of The Silent Partner, *around 1924 (Whyte Museum of the Canadian Rockies)*

(CP)

CHAPTER IV

Hard Times

During the war and the postwar years, the Canadian Pacific hotels suffered greatly from hard times and deterioration of the hotel buildings themselves, some of which had become obsolete. The glorious days of the great hotels in the Rockies came to a halt with the Depression and World War II. After the war, travel changed radically. Aircraft replaced trains and steamships as the most popular means of long-distance transportation. Also, better automobiles changed the way that people travelled. The hotel became more popular with people who were less inclined towards the extravagance and show of wealth displayed by the prewar guests. The new middle-class clientele did not spend fortunes on vacations. By the mid-sixties, the great hotels of the Rockies had become overwhelmingly expensive to maintain. There was talk of selling some of them, and possibly the Chateau Lake Louise. There was even some question of their being demolished.

An enormous amount of work would have to be done if the Chateau was to be saved and there was also an urgent need for new programs. One innovation was the opening of the Chateau in winter for the new skiing clientele. In 1970, Ivor Petrak was made manager of the Banff Springs and Chateau Lake Louise and instructed to breathe new life into both hotels. He embarked on a vast advertising campaign to attract guests to the hotels in the cold winter months. Petrak kept the Banff Springs open during the winter thanks to all sorts of package deals offered at premium rates to entice skiers.

The winter program saved the Banff Springs and the Chateau Lake Louise waited as it opened on a trial basis in the wintertime between 1974 and 1979. During those years, the magazine SKI LIFE printed this appreciation of the ski programs: "Thanks to the efforts of the Banff, Lake Louise and Jasper associates, Canadians are now recognizing their own paradise: a western wilderness of incomparable beauty which offers skiing that can match anything anywhere."

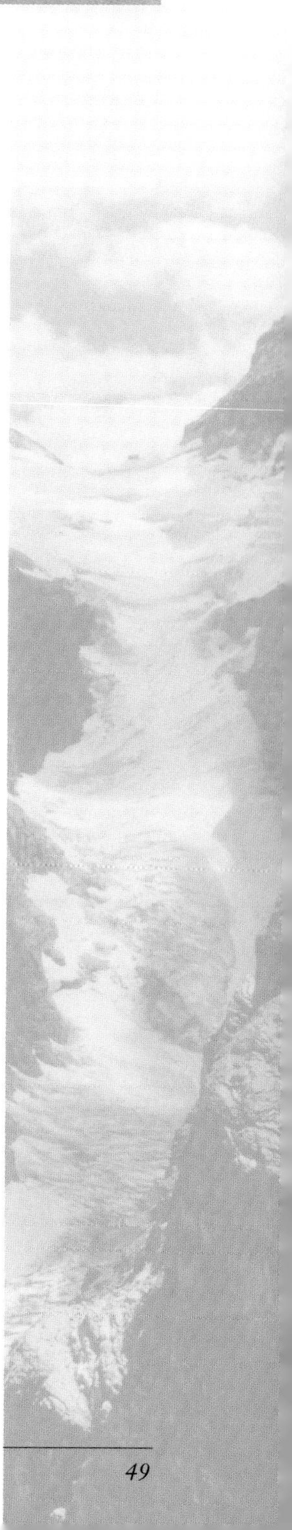

Skiing in the Rockies. Watercolour by W.J. Phillips (CP)

The Chateau remained open to skiers on a trial basis until 1979. Revenues did not justify maintaining such a large building throughout the cold months, so the hotel closed for the winter after that. The Banff Springs Hotel continued to serve skiers, however, and to devise new programs to consolidate their position in the world of ski afficionados.

The winter program lured visitors to the Lake Louise area (CP)

It would not be until 1982 that the Chateau Lake Louise would regain its former glory...

Calgary architects Carruthers and Associates designed the new Glacier Wing, which was completed in 1988 (Carruthers and Associates archives)

CHAPTER V

Entering the New Millennium: A Return to Grandeur

In 1981 William Stinson became president of the Canadian Pacific Railway and chief executive officer in 1985. Stinson was deeply inspired by Van Horne's vision for the railway company and that vision included the restoration and revival of all the company's palatial hotels. He made the decision to upgrade the chateau-like hotels from coast to coast: the Chateau Frontenac, the Laurier, the Royal York, the Palliser, the Banff Springs, the Empress and the Chateau Lake Louise. A new company was formed, Canadian Pacific Hotels and Resorts, with Robert De Mone as president.

The Chateau Lake Louise reopened in winter in 1988. With the Winter Olympics set to be held in Calgary that year, there was a powerful incentive to renovate the hotels in the Rockies. By 1988, the Glacier Wing had been built at Lake Louise. The plans for the Glacier Wing were drawn up by architects Carruthers and Associates of Calgary. The plans show their desire to integrate the new wing into the existing Painter section and the use of corner turrets to repeat the Italianate towers of the 1924 structure.

The new entrance to the Glacier Wing (CPH)

The Carruthers wing and the Painter wing were unified with new rough cast and similar architectural details (R.W. Sandford collection)

The new wing contained 140 more guest rooms, another restaurant, a wine bar and a shopping arcade. Thanks to its 65-million dollar makeover, the Chateau Lake Louise joined the ranks of the CP's sumptuous and grand hotels.

The Glacier Wing extended from the Barrott part of the hotel, with a continuation of its plain walls, and ended in a square tower. The whole Chateau was redone in a new colour—yellow—with new roughcast, or stucco, to unify the different periods of construction. Unfortunately the roofs did not receive the same treatment and the new sections were painted a shade of blue that contrasted badly with the original dark roofs.

(Photos: Timothy Reynolds)

On the ground level, a long covered semi-circular portico housed boutiques and opened into an impressive lobby. From there, broad staircases led to an overhanging balcony around the room and a spectacular chandelier enhanced the opulent atmosphere. Outside, the entrance portico contrasted with the austerity of the overall building: its grand design was much like that used for city hotels.

From the lobby the guests entered a series of large halls continuing on into the redecorated Painter section. In all the rooms, the decorative details and elegant furniture stressed the architects' desire to recreate palatial Swiss chalets. Painted medallions and garlands over all the windows and doorways, contrasting colours to enhance the sculpted ceilings, lighting fixtures featuring antlers and stylized tree branches, and cozy corners and inglenooks all testified to a wish to impart elegance and good taste.

A spectacular chandelier enhanced the opulent atmosphere of the lobby (CPH)

(Photos: Timothy Reynolds)

New restaurants such as the Edelweiss, the Poppy Room, the Tom Wilson and the restored Victoria Dining Room added to the decor. Luxurious suites were built into the new wing with terraces opening high above the breathtaking view of Victoria Glacier. Many new features were added, such as a new pool and sport club.

The original interior decors were being restored in all of the Canadian Pacific's palatial hotels. At Lake Louise, the baronial-style furniture, the new carpeting and appliances, the colour treatment and even the hand-painted archways and windows brought back the hotel's turn-of-the-century elegance. This did not prevent the addition of new plumbing fixtures or electrical upgrading throughout the complex, however. There were also innovations, such as the new shopping arcade.

The restored Victoria Dining Room in the Painter wing (CPH)

So that guests would enjoy their stay at the Chateau even more, the CPR embarked on a vast program of winter activities to attract families and a new clientele to the shores of Lake Louise. A new pamphlet entitled "In the Land of a Million Christmas Trees" vaunted the merits of Lake Louise: "From Bavarian curling on the frozen lake, to dog sled and horse-drawn sleigh rides, to skating parties and to tobogganing and skiing, our wonderland will fill your outdoor time with memory-making moments."

(Photo: France Gagnon Pratte)

The hotel's interior decor enhanced its Victorian atmosphere (CPH)

The lobby recreated the atmosphere of a palatial Swiss chalet (CPH)

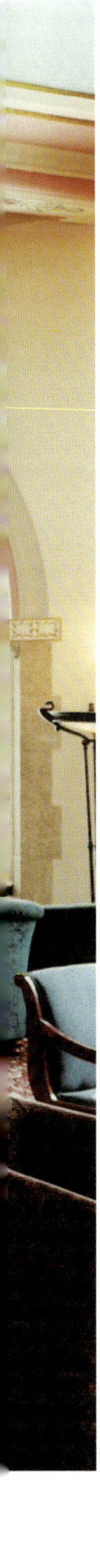

Winter activities attract families (CP)

"In the land of a million Christmas trees", pamphlet in the 1990's (CPH)

The winter scenery at the Chateau was unique. Sparkling snow covered everything and there were lit Christmas trees throughout the winter season. On the Lake, ice sculptures surrounded the skating rink for months. Inside, holly decked the halls from November to January. The "Joy of the Festival of Christmas" delighting young and old alike. Youngsters were especially well treated, what with story time nightly by the fireplace in the Larch lounge over the main lobby. Ice carving demonstrations, fireside carolling, the outdoor Christmas pageant on Christmas Eve, moonlit sleigh rides along the lake and dancing to the sounds of the "Rocky Mountain Rooftop Orchestra" were all pretty hard to beat!

The winter scenery at Chateau Lake Louise is unique (Photo: Karl Weatherly)

(Photo: Karl Weatherly)

Ice carvings and sculptures decked the lake from November to January (Photo: Timothy Reynolds)

(Photo: Timothy Reynolds)

(Photo: Timothy Reynolds)

A great ski resort in the wilderness (CPH)

Skiing at Lake Louise has been called "unspoiled and unforgettable." The World Cup circuit, women's World Cup, Downhill and Super GS have been held there regularly since the 1988 Olympics brought fame to the region. The Lake Louise ski terrain covers more than 4,200 acres and stretches across the faces of four mountains, offering 105 ski runs and 100 kilometres of cross-country skiing trails.

It was really the special winter program that saved Chateau Lake Louise and it is the revamped mountaineering program that sets it apart from the CP's other hotels in the Rockies.

Mountain climbers, painting by C. Rungius (CP)

CHAPTER VI

Lake Louise the Mountaineering Venue

The Lure of the Mountain Tea Houses, Refuges and Camps

The Trail Riders of the Canadian Rockies were founded in 1933 to organize official rides in the mountains (CP)

"A sea of mountains" was the phrase used to describe the great barrier of mountains penetrated by the CPR. Edward Whymper, a celebrated mountain climber who came to the Rockies after conquering the Matterhorn, used the expression "fifty Switzerlands in one." Adjectives like stupendous, gigantic, sublime, colossal and awe-inspiring were often uttered by those who viewed these mountains from the train, and yet they seemed inadequate.

To accommodate mountain climbers, hikers and trail-riders on horseback, the Canadian Pacific built and maintained a series of mountain huts, lodges, or "bungalow camps", and tea houses at various points in the Rockies. Then they advertised the joys of nature:

> In the country for many miles, science has availed itself of nature's gift to create out of the wilderness a mountain park, twenty six miles long by ten wide — a public pleasure ground without equal. Streams have been bridged, roads laid out and trails cut, penetrating for miles into the solitudes so that in several directions the visitor may drive, ride or wander afoot, inhaling the health-giving mountain air, or seeking the most favourable spot for brush, pencil, Kodak, or rod.

The first tea house in the mountains was the Lake Agnes tea house, built in 1901 (CP)

The first refuge to be built was the log cabin on the shores of Lake Louise. It was followed by the tea house at Lake Agnes. Between 1890 and 1930, when the Skoki Lodge was built, in the Chateau Lake Louise area the CPR operated the Lake Agnes Tea House, the Moraine Lake Lodge, the Saddleback Tea House, the Abbot Pass Alpine Hut and the Plain of Six Glaciers Tea House. In addition, the CPR built a number of mountain lodges, sometimes referred to as bungalow camps, which consisted of sleeping cabins and a central dining room and social centre from which the outdoor enthusiast could explore practically virgin territory.

Lake Agnes Tea House

Lake Agnes was first named after a visiting Torontonian, Agnes Cox, in 1890, then christened a second time in honour of Lady Susan Agnes MacDonald, the wife of Canadian Prime Minister Sir John A. MacDonald. Built in 1901 as an added attraction for hikers in the Lake Louise vicinity, the Lake Agnes Tea House was a welcome refuge for visitors climbing to the Lakes in the Clouds as early as 1893. This tea house was a log cabin with a red roof and large verandas overlooking the precipice. Tea was — and still is — served by the stone fireplace. The tea house has been rebuilt over the years and has grown larger but it has kept its romantic design, warm interiors and wonderful location high above the valley below.

The tea house at Lake Agnes today (CPH)

Mountain scene at Moraine Lake; watercolour by A. Sheriff-Scott (CP)

The highest building in Canada, the refuge at Abbott Pass. 1930 (Whyte Museum of the Canadian Rockies)

Moraine Lake Lodge

The Moraine Lake bungalow camp at the head of the Valley of the Ten Peaks was built for mountaineers who came to Lake Louise on horseback. Moraine Lake was discovered by Wilcox and Allen in 1893 but nobody returned until 1899. In 1902, the company built a trail to the area, then a carriage road. Ten years later, the camp was built, a chalet providing food and lodging for the growing number of trekkers. In 1923, a real lodge had to be built and many other buildings and cabins were put up over the years.

Moraine Lake is certainly one of the most magnificent places in the Rockies. The famous mountaineer Walter Wilcox wrote in his guide book: "No scene has ever given me an equal impression of inspiring solitude and rugged grandeur." Moraine Lake itself, which is nine miles from Lake Louise, is two miles long and one-half mile wide, and flanked by a half circle of bare, snow-capped peaks carved and furrowed by glaciers. They are the ten peaks referred to in the Valley of the Ten Peaks and are all over 10,000 feet above sea level. On the other side of the lake are Mount Temple, Pinnacle Peak and Eiffel Peak. Moraine Lake is considered to be as beautiful as Lake Louise, and is often described as such. The exquisitely blue-green water, the peaks soaring up into the sky and the immediacy of the glacier all contribute to form a wild and majestic picture.

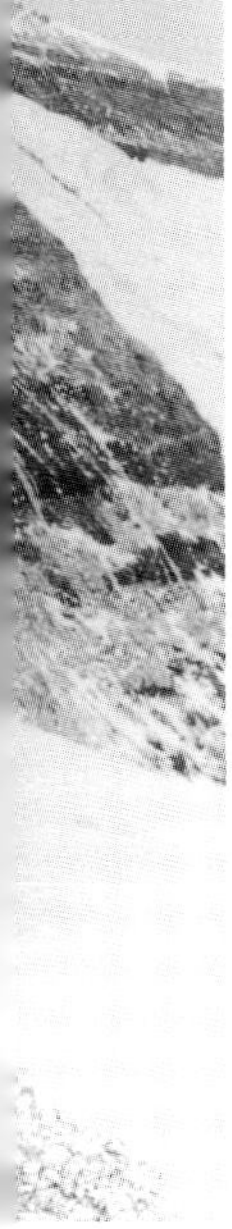

The bungalow camps—clusters of log buildings—are charming. They have a bright, comfortably furnished living and dining room in the main building and are surrounded by several cozy sleeping cabins. These camps, supplemented by tea and rest houses, combine comfort, simplicity and good food in a magnificent natural setting.

CP Poster in the 1930's (CP)

Saddleback Tea House

A tea house was built in Saddleback in 1922, but for its first year only. It was used as a shelter, or "rest house" after that.

The name of the site was chosen in 1894 by Willoughby Astley, the manager of the chalet at Lake Louise, because of its similarity to a saddle, complete with pommel and crupper. Hikers loved the long trail to Saddleback from the shores of Lake Louise, crossing to Paradise Valley and returning by horse trail. From Saddleback there was a wonderful view of the valley and the Temple, Aberdeen and Sheol peaks. Its name, Paradise Valley, was derived from the original Stoney name "Wasback", meaning beautiful. Paradise Valley has six miles of long meadows carpeted with anemones, asters and other alpine flowers. There is a trail from Lake Louise to the rest house on the summit.

Banff and Lake Louise area in the 1930's. Postcard published by the CPR (CP)

Abbot Pass. Photographed by Bruno Engler in 1950.

Abbot Pass Alpine Hut

In the summer of 1922, construction work began on a mountaineers' refuge at Abbot Pass which would become famous as "the highest building in Canada." All the materials had to be taken by packhorse along the bridle path, up to the Plain of Six Glaciers and over the ice to the crevassed area at the bottom of Death Trap. From that point on, all materials, including cement, lime, bolts, windows, timber, stove, tools, beds, mattresses, bedding, cutlery, along with sufficient food to sustain the men while they were at work, had to be carried up the Death Trap on the guides' backs. Their loads weighed up to seventy-five pounds. In 1997, Abbot Hut was commemorated as a national Historic Site.

Plain of Six Glaciers Tea House

The tea house at the Plain of Six Glaciers was built in 1924 by Swiss guides as an overnight shelter for their clients en route to Abbot Pass. The hike from Lake Louise to the Plain of Six Glaciers offers many opportunities for admiring glaciers, and the Mt. Aberdeen Glacier in particular. Every day, as many as 200 to 400 hikers visit the tea house, which has been run by the Smith family since 1961.

In 1900, the CPR pamphlet "The Challenge of the Mountains" lured hikers from the world over to the Canadian west (CP)

Skoki Lodge

Skoki is a Potowatopi Indian name meaning "swamp" and was chosen by Chicago alpinist and surveyor James F. Porter in 1911 as the name, not for a swamp, but for a beautiful valley. The trek took hikers from Lake Louise, up Deception Pass and around Ptarmigan Lake to Skoki Valley. Although the area was covered by hikers from the beginning of the century on, it was the opening of a ski resort in the primeval, almost inaccessible, wilderness that made the area a favourite among mountain lovers. A lodge was finally built in 1930 as the second ski lodge in the Rockies. At 2,160 metres above sea level, it was also the highest guest lodge in the Park.

The author France Gagnon Pratte hiking up Deception Pass to Skoki Valley in the 1950's (Photo: France Gagnon Pratte collection)

Early Alpine Club of Canada climbers, 1930, the President range, Yoho National Park, B.C. (CP)

Peter Sarbach's ice axe was returned to the summit of Mount Lefroy during the centennial celebration of the first ascent of the mountain in 1897 (Photo: Paul Valiulis)

Members of the original August 1897 Mount Lefroy expedition (Alpine Club of Canada)

CHAPTER VII

Birthplace of Canadian Mountaineering

In August 1896, during a small, much publicized expedition to Mount Lefroy, Philip Abbot fell to his death only a few feet away from the summit and became the first man known to have been killed in Canadian mountaineering. The tragic and untimely death of Philip Abbot had a tremendous impact on the climbing community, such as it was in North America. That a well-known and respected climber had given his life to an attempt on Mount Lefroy instantly made both the climber and the mountain famous.

Philip Stanley Abbot, 1890 (Whyte Museum of the Canadian Rockies)

The small expedition and Abbot's death put the Canadian Rockies at the centre of the world mountaineering map. News of the young man's mountaineering death caused a media furor not unlike the one that followed the accident on the Matterhorn in 1865 when four members of Edward Whymper's party fell to their death. Now, however, the shoe was on the North American foot and all the arguments about the legitimacy (and intelligence) of mountaineering as a sport

Stallard party on Asulkan Glacier, July 30, 1897. L. to R: Sam Yovwell, Mrs. Stallard, Dr. Helena Goodwin, George Vaux Jr., Unknown, Dr J.H. Stallard, Harold B. Dixon and Peter Sarbach (Whyte Museum of the Canadian Rockies)

Rescue party on its way to bring down body of Philip Abbot, 1896. L. to R: Tom Wilson, George T. Little, Willoughby Astley (manager of the first chalet at Lake Louise), Charles E. Fay (Whyte Museum of the Canadian Rockies)

surfaced anew. Just as in Europe, the protestations served only to draw attention to the powerful aesthetic which was the basis of the sport. The entire debate only strengthened the argument for ascending and brought new and clear focus to the Canadian Rockies as a world centre for all the important elements that made an alpine experience complete. The Canadian Pacific Railway observed the free advertising with interest. The Rockies had made the news. All that was needed now was to ensure that climbers didn't die in the Rockies. The solution was simple. Amateur climbers needed professional help. The railway would bring European guides to the West and a new era of mountaineering would begin.

The accident had stirred up a real controversy over the necessity of mountaineering in an age when modern technology and evolving cultural sophistication were being applied to the world in such a way as to remove danger and the possibility of unnecessary death from the realm of usual human experience.

On the other hand, one cannot separate what was happening in North America in the late nineteenth century from the heady aesthetics and understated courage that were the hallmarks of British colonialism at the time. Wherever they came from, all true Victorians were bold and daring. They recognized that raw exposure to the bare beauty of empty country was good for the soul. They also looked upon empty landscapes as places where an ambitious ego might be asserted to guarantee a place in posterity.

CPR Swiss guides at Lake Louise circa 1930. L. to R: Ernest Feuz, Rudolph Aemmer, Edward Feuz Jr., Christian Häsler, Walter Feuz (Whyte Museum of the Canadian Rockies)

The man in the hot seat, after the Mount Lefroy accident, was Charles Fay. As president of the Appalachian Mountain Club and a member of the fatal expedition, it fell to him to ensure that Abbot's death was seen in the greater context of the aims of mountaineering.

Charles Fay has offered an articulate and impassioned defense of the nobility of mountaineering that has been used many, many times since. The argument Fay put forward in 1896 has echoed endlessly through all the mountain ranges of the world. Every time a climber dies, Fay's logic is once again evoked to justify the strange and haunting passion which drives men and women skyward into that uncertain vertical world where rock and snow meet sun and storm. A strange calling, climbing is not for everyone. It takes unusual courage to step upward onto the fierce and unforgiving edge. Only a rare few can stare full into the face of gravity's terrible wind.

Arrival of the Guides

Even the most simple and direct mountaineering routes can be fraught with fatal hazard. This is just as true today as it was in August 1896 when Philip Abbot showed that it was easy to die in these mountains, even on standard routes. To climb one has to be fit, experienced, competent and calm. It is apparent that the skills necessary for mountaineering can be acquired in only one of two ways. You can go into the mountains and learn them yourself, through trial and error, with the hope that luck will be on your side – that you won't die or kill someone else in learning. A more practical way is to learn from the experience and wisdom of others. It is this simple concept – that mountaineering can be challenging, gratifying and exhilarating without necessarily being unsafe – that is the basis of the profession of the mountain guide.

It did not take long to persuade the railway that qualified guides would make the mountains safer and more attractive to visitors. CPR officials didn't know how to go about locating competent men in this field, so they approached Thomas Cook, the British travel agency, which had offices in all the major European cities. In the autumn of 1898, contracts were signed between the railway and two Swiss guides from Interlaken, Christian Häsler and Edouard Feuz.

In 1899, the Canadian Pacific Railway brought the first Swiss guides to the Canadian West. With them they brought significant evolutions in mountaineering technique garnered from long experience in the Alps. But, perhaps more importantly, they brought an attitude about mountains and a disposition toward climbing which would gradually change the way many Canadians would think about their own summits.

The Swiss had a reverence for the alpine which would gradually permeate the fabric of Canadian culture. Through the Swiss guides, Canadians would gradually learn the real value of the overwhelming heritage of peaks that nature left behind for hikers and climbers to enjoy. It was the Swiss guides who made manifest the meaning of having so many mountains.

When Feuz and Häsler arrived at Glacier House in the early summer of 1899, they found that, though there were big mountains at Rogers Pass, there were a number of things about them that were very different from what they had grown up with in Switzerland.

Whereas in Switzerland there were elegantly groomed and heavily travelled pathways leading to the bases of the important climbing routes, here there was only the impenetrable bush. Then, too, there was the issue of streams. Great torrents roared forth unbridged from massive, melting glaciers. Guides and their clients teetered across wet and slippery logs or built fragile rafts which they floated, out of control, over the angry waters of swollen rivers. Then there were animals, a hazard which did not exist in the Alps. Though they were only rarely dangerous, elk, moose and deer were highly respected and the big bears were given a wide berth. Even with great care, however, there would be at least one fatal confrontation between guides and grizzlies in the forested valleys that led to the high routes to the peaks.

Another fundamental difference between the European Alps and the mountains of the Canadian West lay in the nature and variety of rock types that could be found in each. Feuz and Häsler had to learn a great deal about the varying terrain of each of the ranges before they could be of full service to their clients. Moreover, all these new obstacles had to be overcome within the confines of the design and weight of contemporary mountaineering gear. It must be clearly noted that the equipment of the day was cumbersome and imperfect.

An expedition on a glacier in the early years of mountain climbing (Whyte Museum of the Canadian Rockies)

But perhaps foremost of all the differences between the Alps of Europe and Canada was the fact that the latter was virtually unpeopled. If a guide or a client got into real trouble, either in the wilderness or on a mountain, there was no one nearby to help. Trained rescue teams did not exist and one could not count on the assistance of other guides or climbers who might be passing by. There weren't any. The mountains of Canada were cold and remote. For all intents and purposes, the summit of a mountain was as distant as the surface of the moon. For a combination of these reasons, guides usually took their clients up the safest and easiest routes, preferring to rely on patience and experience rather than on bravado and unreliable technical aids.

Creation of the Alpine Club of Canada

Swiss guides hired by the railway brought with them far more than evolving new techniques of mountain travel. They also brought with them a new alpine aesthetic that accelerated the developing appreciation of mountains in Canada. To the few Canadians interested in summiteering at the time, they taught rockwork and safety techniques that stimulated a new way of thinking about mountain travel among locals. Mountains were transformed from barriers into destinations in their own right. A mutual respect and reliance developed between climbers like Norman Collie, Peter Sarbach, James Outram and Christian Kaufmann and local guides and outfitters like Tom Wilson, Bill Peyto and Jim Simpson. A truly Canadian alpine aesthetic was developed among these early adventurers and communicated to all that knew them.

In March 1906, the Alpine Club of Canada was founded, with Arthur Oliver Wheeler as President (Whyte Museum of the Canadian Rockies)

One of the first Canadians to be exposed to the burgeoning local alpine aesthetic established by the early European climbers was a young surveyor named Arthur Oliver Wheeler. A tireless champion of a uniquely Canadian sense of the alpine, Wheeler then lobbied hard for the creation of an alpine club in Canada. In March 1906, after all sorts of problems and largely at the instigation of one Elizabeth Parker, the Alpine Club of Canada was founded. Wheeler was elected president and Parker the organization's first secretary.

At last a formal organization existed to incorporate an appreciation of mountains into the evolving culture of this huge new land.

Mountain Guides and the Birth of Western Canadian Skiing

While most returned to Switzerland for the winter, a few Swiss guides were hired by the railway to stay on through the winter months to maintain the empty hotels. Whenever they could they skied, an activity utterly alien to locals who argued that the snowshoe was the only civilized vehicle through the deep powder of the long Canadian winter. Though resident adults in the Rockies considered skiing an outlandish behaviour local children immediately saw the opportunity for fun in the odd new sport introduced by these unusual foreign mountaineers.

There has been much lively debate through the years over which of the early European guides contributed most to the history of mountaineering in Canada. While many point to early Swiss guides who came to Canada to work at Canadian Pacific's mountain hotels, there is also an Austrian contender: Conrad Kain.

In 1908, Kain decided he wanted to leave Austria for the adventure of North America. In preparation he went to Vienna to study English in the home of Erich Pistor, a well-known Viennese climber who had written a fine recommendation to the Canadian Pacific Railway in Canada offering that Kain would make an excellent guide. A representative of the railway had responded that it was too late in the year to make application and that their regular Swiss guides had been engaged. The letter offered, however, that the Alpine Club of Canada might be interested in procuring Kain as a guide. Pistor wrote to A.O. Wheeler who guaranteed Kain a summer job.

The principal reason for Wheeler's invitation to Kain to come to Canada in 1909 was to help him prepare the annual A.C.C. (Alpine Club of Canada) camp to be held at Lake O'Hara. Kain had made a very positive impression on the Alpine Club. He also had a very positive impact on the children of Banff whom he impressed with the fun he had skiing.

By 1920, an informal group of young Banff skiers had created the Banff Ski Club. They began skiing on a logging road on Mt. Norquay and, later, built a small cabin near Norquay Pass. The great success of this first small ski area prompted other explorations for the right combinations of slope and snow and soon Sunshine and Lake Louise were included in the expanding adventure that was skiing in the Bow Valley. As interest in the sport grew so did the demand for mechanization that would reduce the time spent climbing as opposed to real skiing. A hundred years after the arrival of the first professional mountain guide in Canada, downhill and cross-country skiing have become national pastimes attracting more than a million people to the Rockies each winter. Professional mountain guides can take real pride in the fact they helped make Canada into a skiing nation.

In 1939, Bruno Engler came from Switzerland to the Canadian Rockies and began working as a mountain guide at Lake Louise and ski instructor at Sunshine Village. He is a living legend as a photographer, cinematographer, mountain man, storyteller and « Bon vivant » (Photo: R. Faure)

CPR Swiss guide Ernest Feuz and Georgia Englehard climbing Mount Victoria Glacier, July 21st, 1936 (CP)

CONCLUSION

In their luxurious suite overlooking Victoria Glacier, guests dream of mountain climbing (CP)

Lake Louise and Canadian Alpine Culture

When the famous mountaineer Philip Abbot fell off Mt.Lefroy in the summer of 1896, many in Canada wanted to ban climbing. In response, Canadian Pacific Railway wisely chose to bring professional guides to its mountain hotels to teach guests how to climb the high peaks safely. These competent professionals taught generations of Canadians how to climb as well as how to ski. In so doing they helped establish a distinctly Canadian alpine culture and centred it in the country's western mountains. Over a century this culture has rooted and grown. Now Canada is one of the best known alpine countries in the world, a fact substantiated in 1996 when the International Federation of Mountain Guides Associations held their annual meeting.

Canadian Pacific Hotels strives to constantly upgrade its historical place in the western mountain parks. Its great properties there could only survive, however, if they opened year round. In order to attract customers, these old hotels had to turn their back on their heritage so as to be able to gradually afford to restore these magnificent heritage buildings to their former grandeur. Thirty years and 250 million dollars in improvements later, Canadian Pacific is now ready to return to its original roots.

Now that its national park properties are once again leading luxury resort hotels, Canadian Pacific is returning to its traditional landscape heritage. Canadian Pacific is presently improving service and decreasing the number of rooms in key national park properties so as to attract the discriminating international clientele whose central interests focus around the experience of nature. As a concluding element of this restoration program, Canadian Pacific has re-created the time-honoured tradition of offering mountain guiding services at its mountain national park hotels.

In the summer of 1997, on the centennial anniversary of the arrival of the first Swiss guides in the Canadian Rockies, Canadian Pacific restored its mountaineering program at the Chateau Lake Louise and its other mountain national park properties. Through the re-introduction of the mountain guiding tradition, Canadian Pacific hopes to return again to that golden age of exploration and adventure when it was a principal partner in celebrating the highest and best use of our national parks.

For over a hundred years, the Chateau Lake Louise has offered elegance, exquisite cuisine and gracious hospitality on the shores of the most spectacular mountain lake in the world. It is indeed a diamond in the wilderness:

> "Nestling at the foot of two great mountains which seem to guard against the encroachments of the vast glaciers resting on the sides of a third, canopied by a sky like the petal of a soft blush rose, its unfathomable waters reproducing, with mirror-like fidelity, the green forests, bare peaks and motionless seas of snow-mantled ice — Lake Louise is a dream of loveliness."

Bibliography

Archives

Chateau Lake Louise Archives, Lake Louise

Canadian Pacific Hotels Archives, Montreal.

Canadian Pacific Railway Archives Company, Montreal

Globe and Mail Archives, Toronto

McGill University Archives, Montreal

Whyte Museum of the Canadian Rockies Archives, Banff

Books

Beers, Don *The World of Lake Louise.* Calgary: Highline Publishing, 1996

Berton, Pierre *The Last Spike.* Toronto: McClelland & Stewart, 1971

Choko, Mark and David L. Jones *Canadian Pacific Posters, 1883-1963.* Montreal: Meridian Press, 1988

Gagnon Pratte, France and Eric Etter *The Chateau Frontenac. One Hundred Years in the Life of a Legendary Hotel* Québec: Continuité Press, 1993

Gagnon Pratte, France *The Banff Springs Hotel, A Castle in the Rockies.* Québec: Continuité Press, 1998

Gagnon Pratte, France *Country Houses for Montrealers.The Architecture of Edward and W.S. Maxwell. 1892-1924.* Montreal: Meridian Press, 1987.

Hart, E.J. *The Selling of Canada, The CPR and the Beginnings of Canadian Tourism.* Banff: Altitude Publishing, 1983

Kalman, Harold D. *A History of Canadian Architeture, Vol I and II.* Toronto: Oxford University Press, 1994

Kalman, Harold D. *The Railway Hotels and the Development of the Chateau Style in Canada.* Victoria, B.C: University of Victoria, 1968

Lamb, Kaye *History of the Canadian Pacific.* New York: McMillan Pub. Co., 1977

Lavallée, Omer *Van Horne Road.* Montreal: Railfare Book, 1974

Mayles, Stephen *William Van Horne.* Don Mills, Ont: Fitzhenry & Whiteside, 1983

Pole, Graeme *The Canadian Rockies.* Banff: Altitude Publishing, 1991

Sandford, R.W. *At the Top: 100 Years of Mountain Guiding in Canada.* Canmore: The Alpine Club of Canada, 1996

Sandford, R.W. *The Book of Banff.* Banff: The Friends of Banff, 1994

Sandford, R.W. and Geoff Powter *Canadian Summits.* Canmore: The Alpine Club of Canada, 1995

Sandford, R.W. *The Canadian Alps: The History of Mountaineering in Canada.* Banff: Altitude Publishing, 1989

Vaughan, Walter *The Life and Work of Sir William Van Horne.* New York: The Century Company, 1920

Whyte, Jon and E. Cavell *Rocky Mountain Madness.* Banff: Altitude Publishing, 1982

Whyte, Jon and Carole Harmon *Lake Louise, A Diamond in the Wilderness.* Banff: Altitude Publishing, 1982

Periodicals

Caraffe, Marc and Janet Wright "Les hôtels de style château des compagnies ferroviaires" Agenda paper. Historic Sites and Monuments Board of Canada, 1980

Construction, April 1926

Léon, Maurice "Lake Louise. Causerie d'outre-mer" in *Le Figaro,* Paris, Sept 26, 1910.